Super Sea Creatures

SEA SNAKES

GAIL TERP

BLACK RABBIT BOOKS

Bolt is published by Black Rabbit Books
P.O. Box 3263, Mankato, Minnesota, 56002.
www.blackrabbitbooks.com

Marysa Storm, editor; Grant Gould, designer;
Omay Ayres, photo researcher

Names: Terp, Gail, 1951- author.
Title: Sea snakes / by Gail Terp.
Description: Mankato, Minnesota : Black Rabbit Books, [2021] | Series: Bolt. super sea creatures | Includes bibliographical references and index. | Audience: Ages 8-12 | Audience: Grades 4-6 | Summary: "Dive into learning about sea snakes with vibrant photography, engaging text, and range maps, size comparisons, and other infographics"– Provided by publisher. Identifiers: LCCN 2019026832 (print) | LCCN 2019026833 (ebook) | ISBN 9781623102869 (hardcover) | ISBN 9781644663820 (paperback) | ISBN 9781623103804 (ebook)
Subjects: LCSH: Sea snakes–Juvenile literature.
Classification: LCC QL666.O64 T47 2021 (print) | LCC QL666.O64 (ebook) | DDC 597.96/5–dc23
LC record available at https://lccn.loc.gov/2019026832
LC ebook record available at https://lccn.loc.gov/2019026833

Printed in the United States. 2/20

Image Credits

Alamy: BIOSPHOTO, 28–29; Brandon Cole Marine Photography, 18; Doug Perrine, 4–5; ephotocorp, 32; Poelzer Wolfgang, 8; Stocktrek Images, Inc., 15; bdi.conabio.gob.mx: Iván Lira Torres, 31; BluePlanetArchive.com: Clay Bryce, 12; Nigel Marsh, 9; californiaherps.com: California Herps, 22–23; commons.wikimedia.org: Aloaiza, 16–17 (bkgd); faculty.sdmiraramar.edu: Elisse Tallerico, 1, 6–7; iStock: CoreyFord, 24 (shark); Ken Griffiths, 20–21; Shutterphuma, 24 (btm eel); ValentynVolkov, 24 (eggs); Minden: Colin Marshall, 26–27; Jurgen Freund, Cover (snake); oceana.org: Oceana, 3; Shutterstock: blue-sea.cz, Cover (bkgd); Evlakhov Valeriy, 24 (top eel, fish); poorbike, 16–17 (silhouettes), 24 (sea snake); Sergey Uryadnikov, 24 (sea eagle); tropicalherping.com: Tropical Herping, 10–11; tumblr.com: todropscience, 23

CONTENTS

CHAPTER 1

IN THE SEA

A small fish hides in a coral reef. Nearby, a sea snake swims. The snake pokes its head in the reef's cracks and holes. It's getting closer and closer to the fish. Soon, it pokes its head in the fish's hole. Quickly, the snake grabs the fish and **injects venom** with its fangs. It waits for the squirming fish to go still. Then the snake eats it and swims on.

COMPARING LENGTHS

olive sea snake

yellow-bellied sea snake

turtle-headed sea snake

dusky sea snake

feet

Sea Snake Bodies

Sea snakes swim in some of the world's oceans. There are more than 50 kinds of them. They spend their lives at sea. They have long, narrow bodies. Their tails are flattened like a paddle. This shape helps them swim quickly.

Sea snakes come in many colors and patterns. Colors include black, brown, and yellow. Most have patterns of colored bands. Each type looks different.

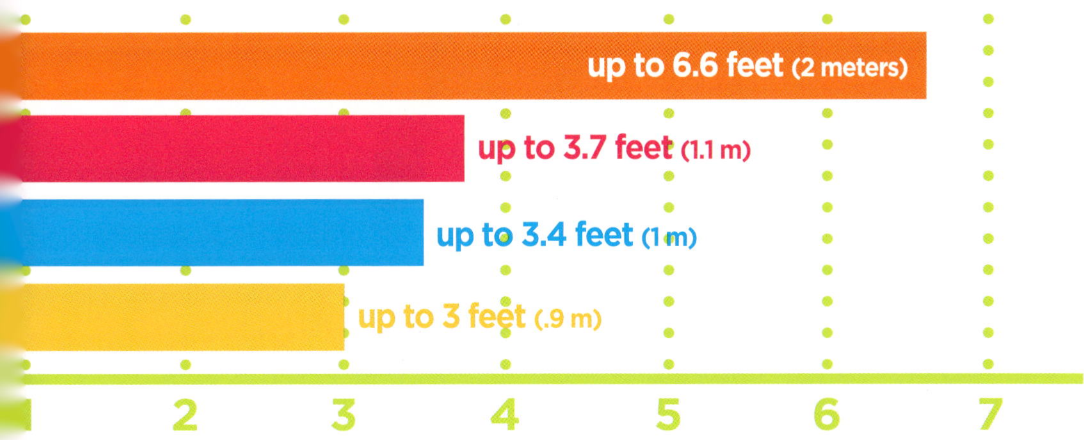

Breathing

Sea snakes breathe through nostrils. To breathe, the snakes swim to the water's surface. The nostrils close up when they dive back down. Water cannot get in. While they swim, the snakes' skin takes in **oxygen** from the water. This action lets them stay underwater longer.

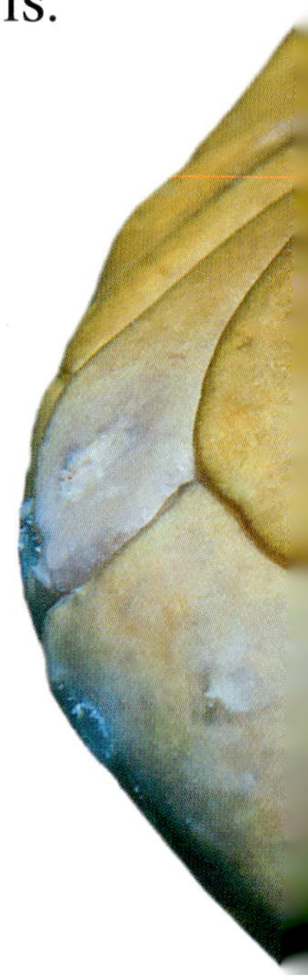

Barnacles often stick onto sea snake skin. Sea snakes shed their skin often to get rid of them.

SEA SNAKE FEATURES

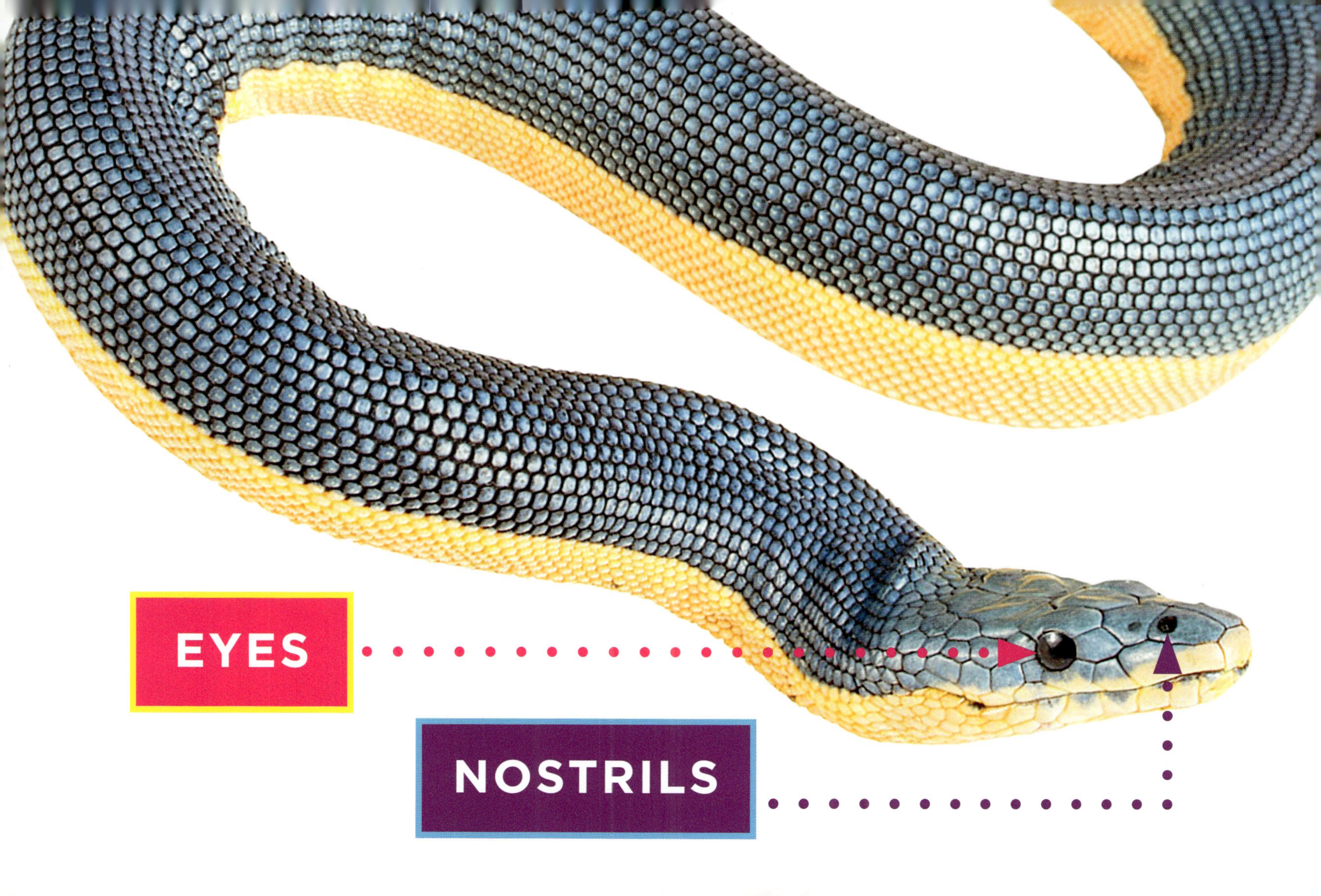
EYES
NOSTRILS

Sea snakes are active during the day and night.

CHAPTER 2

FOOD TO EAT and a Place to Live

Sea snakes are excellent hunters. Common **prey** includes fish, fish eggs, and moray eels. Sea snakes search for prey near the ocean floor. Once they find prey, they bite it. Then they inject it with venom. Soon, the animal can't move. The snakes then swallow the prey whole.

Habitat

Sea snakes are found in the Pacific and Indian Oceans. Most live along shallow **coasts**. They often swim through coral reefs or among seagrass. Yellow-bellied sea snakes are the only kind that live in the open sea.

WHERE SEA SNAKES LIVE

Sea Snake Range Map

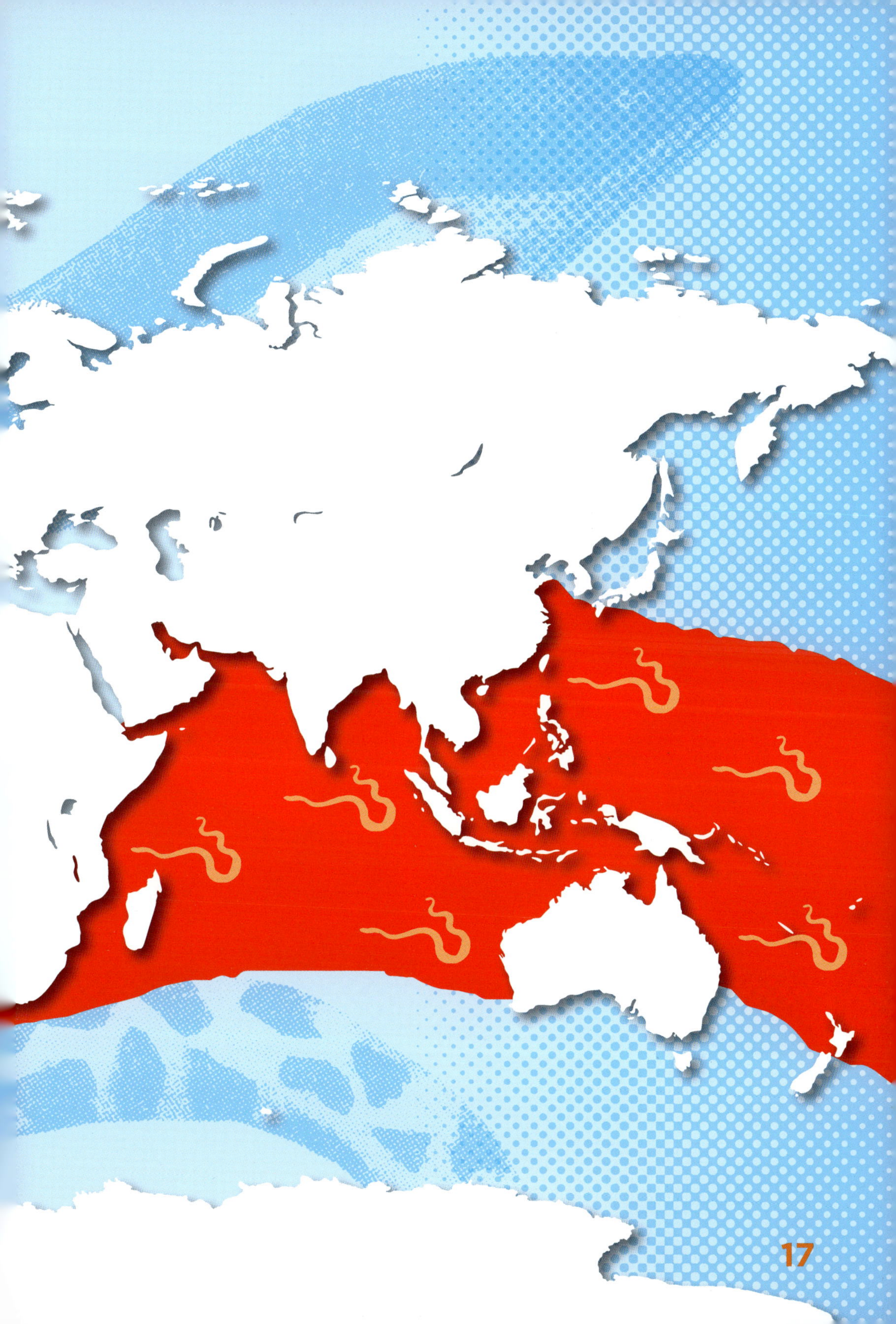

Most female sea snakes have babies once a year.

CHAPTER 3

FAMILY LIFE

Sea snakes mostly live and hunt alone. Sometimes, they gather in groups. Scientists think these groups might form when it's time to **mate**. Different types of sea snakes mate at different times of year.

On Their Own

Four to 11 months after mating, females give birth to babies. Right away, the babies swim to the surface. They take their first breaths. The baby snakes are on their own. Mother sea snakes don't help take care of them.

'5 to .85 foot (.23 to .26 m)

up to 3.7 feet (1.1 m)

2 3 4

BY THE NUMBERS

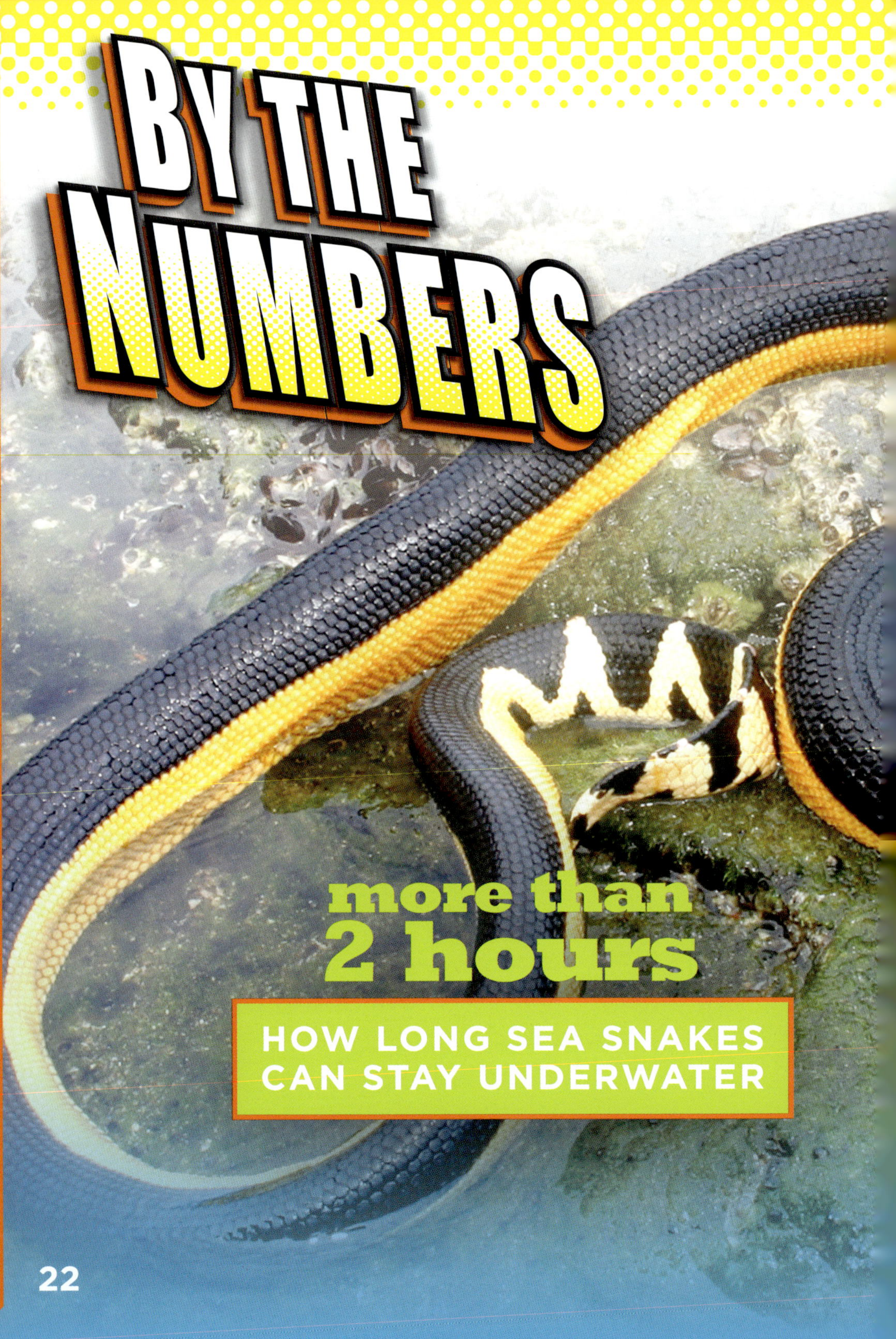

more than 2 hours

HOW LONG SEA SNAKES CAN STAY UNDERWATER

EVERY
2 TO 6 WEEKS
HOW OFTEN SEA SNAKES SHED

2 to 9
AVERAGE NUMBER OF BABIES FEMALE SEA SNAKES HAVE AT ONE TIME

up to 328 feet (100 m)
HOW DEEP SOME SEA SNAKES CAN DIVE

Sea Snake Food Chain

This food chain shows what eats sea snakes. It also shows what sea snakes eat.

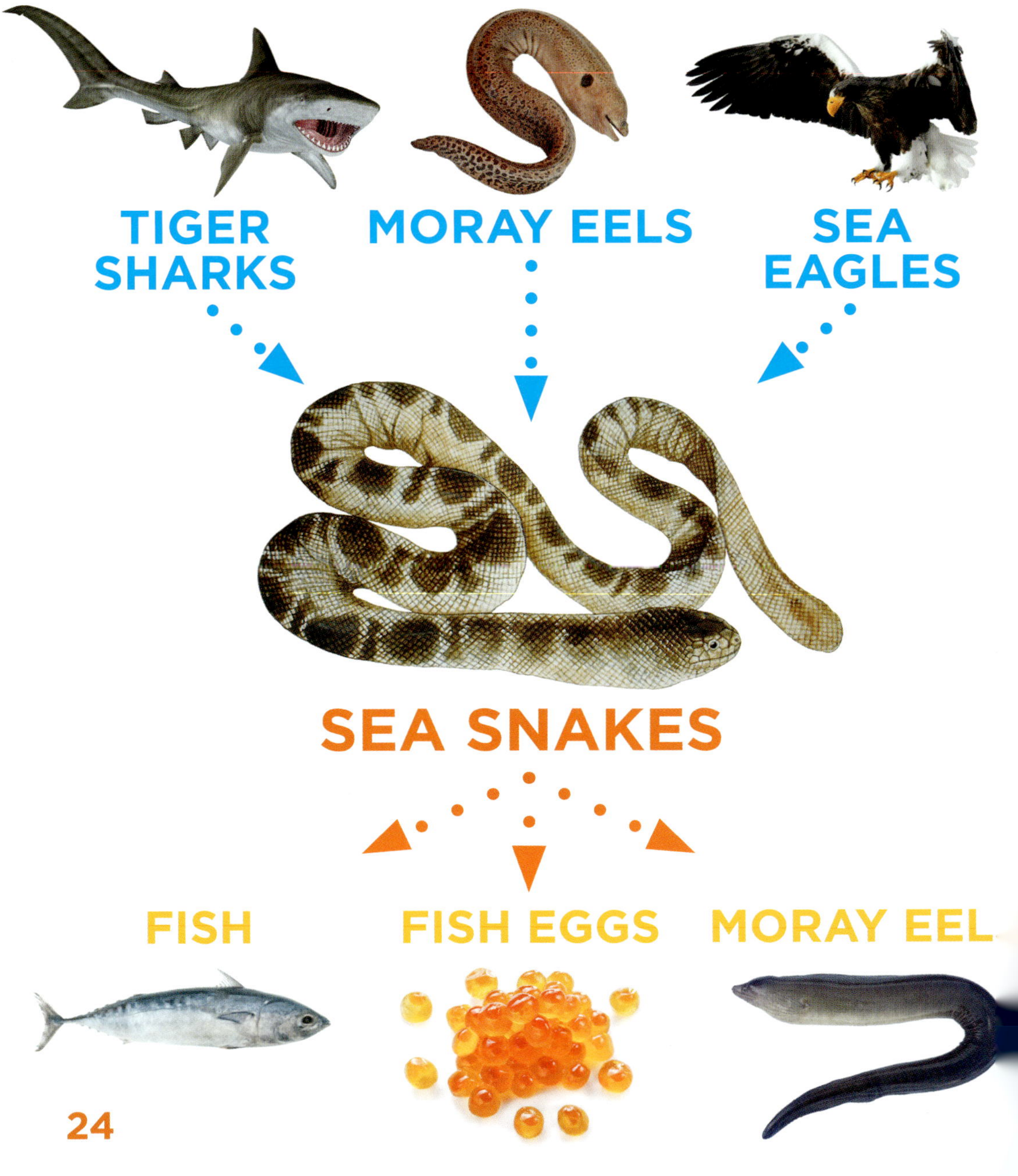

CHAPTER 4

Part of THEIR WORLD

Sea snakes are faced with many threats. Large fish and moray eels eat them. So do tiger sharks and sea eagles.

Sea snakes can protect themselves, though. They can swim away from danger. They hide in rocks and coral reefs. They also attack with venom.

Medicine from Venom

Some people, such as Bryan Fry, study snake venom. They want to know how the venom works. Not all sea snake venom is the same. Some types attack preys' brains. Some types hurt other body parts. Fry hopes to use what he learns about venom to make medicine.

Sea snakes are shy. They rarely attack humans.

A Big Part

Some sea snakes are in danger. Humans overhunt them. **Pollution** and **climate change** hurt sea snakes' homes too. These snakes might die out. It's up to people to help them.

Sea snakes are an important part of the ocean. They eat many animals. They help feed other animals too. Someday, their venom might help make medicine. These animals truly are super sea creatures.

GLOSSARY

barnacle (BAHR-nuh-kuhl)—a kind of small shellfish that attaches itself to rocks, the bottoms of boats underwater, and some animals

climate change (KLAHY-mit CHEYNJ)—changes in the earth's weather patterns

coast (KOHST)—the land near a shore

inject (IN-jekt)—to force a liquid into something

mate (MAYT)—to join together to produce young

oxygen (AHK-si-jin)—a gas that is necessary for life

pollution (puh-LOO-shun)—substances that make land, water, or air dirty and not safe to use

prey (PRAY)—an animal hunted or killed for food

shed (SHED)—to lose or cast aside a natural covering or part

venom (VEH-num)—a poison made by animals used to kill or injure

LEARN MORE

BOOKS

Fortescue, Madeleine. *Deadly Animal Poisons.* Ultimate Animal Defenses. New York: Gareth Stevens Publishing, 2017.

Hirschmann, Kris. *Deadliest Snakes.* Deadliest Predators. San Diego: ReferencePoint Press, Inc., 2017.

Shaffer, Lindsay. *Sea Snakes.* Animals of the Coral Reef. Minneapolis: Bellwether Media, Inc., 2020.

WEBSITES

Sea Snakes
animalcorner.co.uk/animals/sea-snakes/

Sea Snakes Facts and Information
seaworld.org/animals/facts/reptiles/sea-snakes/

Super Snakes
kids.nationalgeographic.com/explore/nature/super-snakes/

INDEX